LORNA
HAVE FUN

First Published in Great Britain in 2005 by
Frankly Sweet Publications

Distributor - Search Press Limited
Wellwood, North Farm Road,
Tunbridge Wells, Kent TN2 3DR

REVISED EDITION 2010

©Frances McNaughton 2005

ISBN 978-0-9549761-2-5

Design by Frances McNaughton
Photography by Mike Kelly

Printed in Malaysia

To my Husband Mike,
Thanks for all your love and support in making this book.

And with many thanks to Chelin Miller
and Mike Hutchinson for their help with
proof-reading.

Modelling Fairies In Sugar

By
Frances McNaughton

FSP
Family Sweet
Publications

Contents

Foreword

Having known Frances for some 12 years or so, it gives me great pleasure to introduce her new book. Anyone who enjoys Sugarcraft will take pleasure in both the subject matter and Frances' enthusiasm for her subject.

Frances is one of our most popular demonstrators and having seen myself the patience and attention to detail that she displays during her demonstrations, it is easy to see why. She gives encouragement and motivation to all her students during her home based classes ensuring that each pupil leaves with a finished piece to be proud of. Her visiting demonstrations leave her very much in demand. Her sense of humour and willingness to stay long after the session ends to discuss the finer points of her craft making her very popular indeed.

I believe that this long awaited book will continue to bring Frances' skills and professional approach to many more lovers of Sugarcraft. I am sure that her fans will enjoy the subject, the delightful photographs and the easy step by step guide to producing an array of many wonderful pieces

Eddie Spence MBE

February 2005

Introduction

In writing this book, my intention is to introduce each fairy to you in the same way I would teach it in a class. Every fairy is set out in the order I would make it, not necessarily allowing any item to dry unless stated. The idea is that you will be able to make a whole fairy in one sitting, without the need to leave stages to dry overnight. For this reason I use wires as supports. This of course means that they are not intended to be eaten (after all, who would want to eat a fairy?) but are safe to be used for cake decoration, or simply kept as a display piece.

I have tried to keep the materials as simple as possible. Using commercially bought Flowerpaste and Mexican Paste, and by using paste and powder colours as the original colour, should help those of you who may be a bit nervous about mixing. Sugarpaste and Royal Icing are also available commercially. I have included a recipe for Mexican paste on page 94.

I hope that this book inspires you to make fairies of your own. I have set it out in such a way that the fairies can be adapted to your own design using different heads or dressing in different petals to the ones shown. The instructions can also be utilised with other modelling pastes (e.g. Cold porcelain, or Polymer Clay).

The scenery photographed for the fairies was taken in Scotland - a place known for its sightings of real fairies - by my husband, Mike in 2004. Unfortunately the pictures of the *real* fairies did not come out, so I had to super-impose my own sugar fairies in their place for use in the book!

Basic Tools and Materials

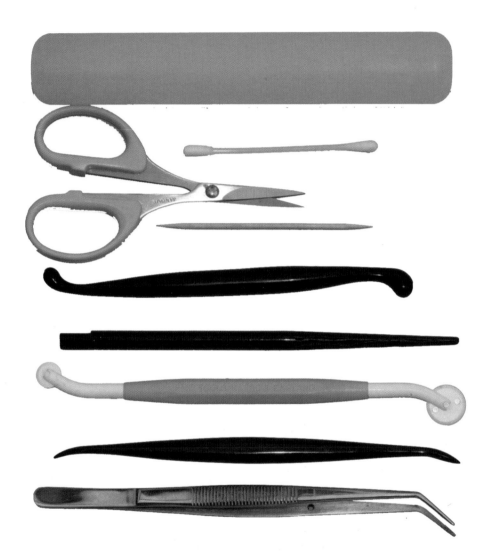

Non-stick Rolling Pin

Cheap Cotton Buds

Sharp Pointed Scissors

Cocktail Sticks

Dogbone Tool

Jem Petal Veiner

PME Cutting Wheel

Dresden Tool

Tweezers

You will also need a non-stick board for rolling out flowerpaste. I use a dark coloured, Corian board rubbed with a little vegetable oil.

The other tools I used in this book are:

0000 (Very fine!) paintbrush
7/16 Dusting Brushes
Wire Cutters

Double-sided silicone veiners:
Poppy Petal
Alstromeria
Hydrangea/ general leaf veiner
Garden Rose
Fruit and Nut

Paper Covered Craft Wires:
White 33g
White 24g
White 18g

Materials:
Mexican Paste
Flowerpaste (or 50%Mexican paste +
50% Sugarpaste)
Confectioners varnish
Leaf Glaze (50% Confectioners Glaze & 50% Isopropyl Alcohol)
Royal Icing
Ready-made Sugarpaste
Alcohol for painting (I used Isopropyl)
Sugarflair Paste Colours -
    Paprika, Christmas Green, Eucalyptus, Christmas Red, Melon, and Grape Violet
Sugarflair Powder Colours -
    Melon, Egg Yellow, Dusky Pink, Brown, Nutkin Brown, Deep Purple, Foliage Green,
    Autumn Leaf, Eucalyptus, Plum, Cornish Cream, Black, Pearl White.
Food-safe non-toxic Glitters

Holly Products Head Moulds:
Fairy Heads
Fairy/Elf
Baby/Child/Boy

Cutters:
Butterfly Wings (Various)
Rose Petals (Various sizes)
Rose Leaves
Periwinkle Leaves
Sweet Pea (2 sizes)
Calyx (Various sizes)
Carnation Medium
Small six-petal Cutters
Small five-Petal Cutters
Primrose Cutters
Holly Leaf Small
Plunger Blossoms
Heart Cutter
Maple leaf Cutter
Garrett Frill Cutter

Florist Tape:
Green, Twig, White

SleepingBabyFairy

Bed Of Rose Leaves

Roll out flowerpaste finely - allow surface to dry for a few minutes.

Take a small ball of flowerpaste and insert a dry white 33g wire a distance equal to the length of the Rose leaf cutter. Squeeze firmly and roll back up to the tip of the wire.

Place under a plastic sheet while preparing the rest of the wires, making one for each leaf.

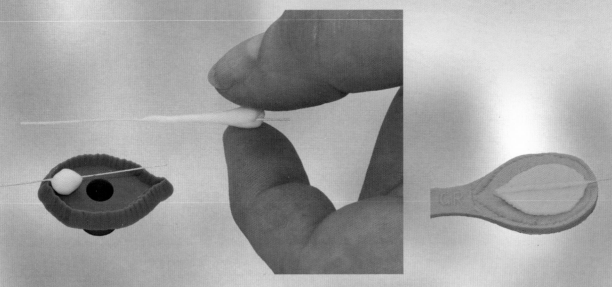

Flip rolled-out paste over, cut out at least seven.

Press a paste-covered wire on each leaf, right to the tip of the leaf.

Lay each leaf on a Rose leaf veiner, wire-side onto the back face of the veiner helping to form the vein on the back.

Press very firmly with the other half of the veiner - this will fix the wire to the leaf. Repeat with the remaining leaves.

Colour each leaf by brushing with Foliage Green powder.
Dip the leaves into Leaf Glaze and blot straight-away on tissue.

Tape the wires together with quarter-width florist tape as soon as the glaze has evaporated and form a bunch of leaves which can be opened to form a flat circle.
Cut the wires to 2cm. Bend the wire flat under the leaves. Shape to make a bed for the baby to sleep on with the wire side underneath.
Paint another coat of Leaf Glaze onto the leaves to give a realistic sheen (use a cotton bud dipped in leaf glaze to save damaging paintbrushes).

Baby Fairy

Use Mexican paste, or a mixture of Mexican and sugarpaste, with a tiny amount of Paprika food colour paste.

Head

Make a smooth 1cm ball of Flesh-coloured Mexican paste.
Shape ball to form a short cone with a point.
Gently rub a small amount of cornflour over the surface.

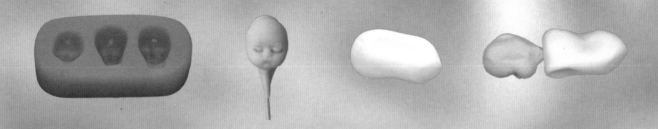

Push cone into the small Baby Head mould (Holly Products) with the point into the nose.
Lay a 4cm 18g wire, or a cocktail stick on top the paste and push the paste and wire into the mould with the end of a small rolling pin.
Keeping the head in the mould, bring the spare paste together to form the back of the head and lift head out of mould. Cut off excess paste with scissors. Shape the neck by smoothing it down the wire.
Paint features on the baby's face with soft, pale brown colour using a very fine brush and Brown powder mixed with alcohol. Paint a single curve along the lower edge of each eye for the closed eyes, and another single curve for each eyebrow.
Paint a very thin line across the lips using a soft Dusky Pink mixed with alcohol.

Body

Form white Mexican paste into a 1.5cm smooth ball. Use little finger to roll across the ball to form a waist. Holding finger on top of the shoulder, push dogbone tool up to form arm sockets and shoulders. Pinch to form leg sockets. Remove the wire from the head and attach head to body with head turned slightly to one side leaving a small amount of neck showing under head.

Finished baby will be lying on her front with head turned to one side.

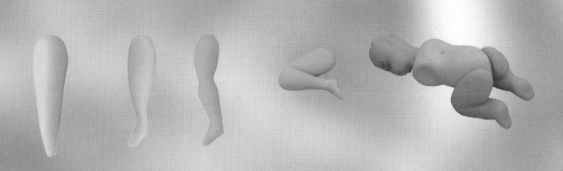

Legs

Make both legs at the same time to ensure they are the same size. Make two smooth 1cm balls of Flesh-coloured Mexican Paste and put one under plastic while working on the other. Roll each to form long carrot-shape approximately the combined length of the head and body. A short way from narrow end, roll between two fingers to form an indent for ankle. Half-way between ankle and top of thigh roll between two fingers. Bend leg and pinch front of knee. Baby is kneeling right down, so knee should be bent tightly. Bend the foot forward and pinch to form a heel. Attach legs by moistening leg sockets with water.

Frilly Knickers

Pipe frilly knickers with white royal icing using either No.1.5 or Ribbon No.31R (PME) piping tube. First pipe the outside edge to get the shape correct, then fill in with tiny zig-zag movements to look frilly.

Arms

Start the same way as for making the legs. Make both arms at the same time to ensure they are the same size. Make two smooth pea-size 1cm pieces and put one of them under plastic while working on the other. Roll each to form long carrot-shape slightly longer than the body. A short way from the narrow end, roll between two fingers to form an indent for the wrist.

Half-way between the wrist and top of arm roll between two fingers.Bend arm and pinch to form elbow. Flatten hand and cut out a tiny triangle of paste on one side to form a mitten shape. Smooth cut edge and curl hand over with thumb sticking out. Remember to make a left and right hand.

Clothes

All made with flowerpaste, rolled very thinly, left to dry slightly before turning over to cut out pieces. Cut out at least seven small 1.5cm rose petals. Soften edges by rolling with JEM petal veiner. Attach the small rose petals while royal icing is still soft to form a short skirt.

Bodice

Roll out flowerpaste again to cut out tiny rose leaves. Press into Garden Rose leaf veiner and colour each leaf by brushing with Foliage Green powder. Attach to body by moistening with water starting at the waist, with the point down over the top of the petals. Keep adding leaves, sticking them round top half of the body until she is fully dressed.

Sleeve

Roll out flowerpaste. Cut out Small Calyx/Jasmine and colour each by brushing with Foliage Green powder.

Attach Arms

Stick Calyx/Jasmine into each arm socket. Then attach arms into sockets, positioning them with elbows at waist and hands towards head. Thumbs near the head, she can be made to look like she is sucking her thumb. Bring calyx over top of arms to look like short sleeves.

Bonnet

Use a small 5-petal cutter to cut out and frill a flower and place the tiny rose petals around head to look like a baby's bonnet, with the petals slightly hiding the face.

Form flowerpaste to a 'Mexican Hat', cut out a Calyx/Jasmine. Colour by brushing with Foliage Green powder. Thin each point of the calyx with the Jem petal veiner. Curve the tail of the calyx.

Dampen underside of calyx and attach to back of head on top of the frilled flower.

Wings

Roll out flowerpaste and cut out a Tiny Butterfly. Frill the edges. Make an indentation down the centre with the blunt side of a knife. Paint or dust with Pearl White colour. Leave to set for a short time with edges propped up in folded paper. When dry enough to handle, stick to the back of the fairy with a small amount of Royal Icing or 'Gunge' (a small amount of flowerpaste mixed with water to form a tacky paste). Prop up wings until dry.

Sleeping Rose Fairy

Bed Of Rose Petals

(I have made the rose petals with wires, but if you prefer to make petals without wires follow the instructions for colouring and veining and stick the petals together. Prop up edges of petals with cotton wool or tissue until set)

Wired Method: Roll out flowerpaste finely - allow surface to dry for a few minutes. Take a small ball of flowerpaste and insert a dry white 33g wire a distance equal to the length of a 5cm Rose Petal cutter. Squeeze firmly and roll back up to the tip of the wire. Place under a plastic sheet while preparing the rest of the wires, making one for each petal. Flip the rolled-out paste over, cut out five petals. Press a paste-covered wire on each petal, right to the edge of the petal.

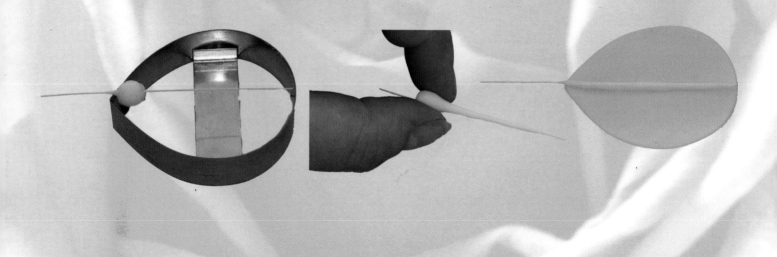

Lay each petal on a Poppy Petal veiner. Press very firmly with the other half of the veiner. This will fix the wire to the petal. Repeat with the remaining petals. Colour each petal by brushing with powder. I used Plum on the edges, Cornish Cream at the stem end. Thin the edge by rolling with a JEM petal veiner.

Tape wires together with quarter-width florist tape form a bunch of petals which can be opened to form a flat circle. Cut the wires to 2cm. Bend the cut wire flat under the petals. With the wire side underneath the flower, make a bed with curved-up petals for the fairy to sleep on. The edges of the petals can be shaped by rolling the edge back over a cocktail stick.

25

Head

Make a smooth ball of Flesh-coloured Mexican paste approximately 1cm.

Shape to form a short cone with a point.

Gently rub a small amount of cornflour over the surface.

Push into the Large Fairy head mould (Holly Products) with the point into the nose.

Lay a 4cm 18g wire or cocktail stick on top the paste and push the paste and wire into the mould with the end of a small rolling pin.

Keeping the head in the mould bring the spare paste together to form the back of the head and lift head out of mould. Cut off excess paste with scissors. Shape the neck by smoothing it down the wire.

Paint features on the fairy's face using a very fine brush (0000) and brown powder mixed with alcohol for the closed eyes - paint a single curve along the lower edge of each eye, and another single curve for each eyebrow.
Keep the brown pale, as it will look more natural. Paint a very thin line across the lips using a soft dusky pink.

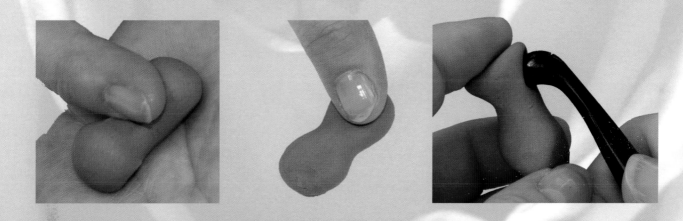

Body

Form Green Mexican paste into a 2cm smooth ball. Use little finger to roll across the ball to form a waist. Holding finger on top of the shoulder, push dogbone tool in and up to form arm sockets and shoulders. Pinch to form leg sockets. Cut the wire in the head shorter than the body or gently remove the wire if preferred. Attach head to body by moistening the neck, and leaving a small amount of neck showing under head. Curve into position to lie on her side.

Legs

Make both legs at the same time to ensure they are the same size. Make two smooth 1.5cm balls of Flesh-coloured Mexican Paste and put one under a plastic sheet while working on the other. Roll each to form long carrot-shape approximately the combined length of the head and body. A short way from narrow end, roll between two fingers to form an indent for ankle. Half-way between ankle and top of thigh roll between two fingers. Bend leg and pinch front of the knee. Bend the foot forward and pinch to form a heel.

Stick into position by moistening the leg sockets with water. Bend the knees to fit within the flower.

Skirt

Cut out at least five rose petals from rolled-out flowerpaste to form the skirt. Powder colour each one. Thin each petal by rolling with a Jem petal veiner. Attach rose petals around waist with a damp paintbrush to form a skirt. Stick the body to the Open Rose Bed with a small amount of Royal Icing.

Bodice

Roll out flowerpaste finely. Cut out at least five rose leaves (depending on the size you are using) to form the waistcoat. Press into garden rose leaf veiner. Powder colour each one. I used foliage green. Attach to the body with the points coming down over the top of the petal skirt.

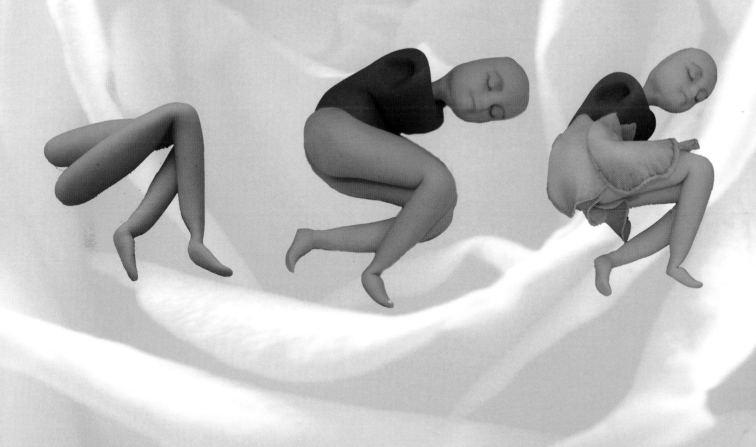

Arms

Make both arms at the same time to ensure they are the same size. Make two smooth 1cm balls of Mexican paste coloured with Paprika food colour paste. Put one of them under plastic while working on the other. Roll each ball to form long carrot-shape approximately the length of the body and half the head. A short way from the narrow end, roll between two fingers to form an indent for the wrist. Half-way between the wrist and top of arm, roll between two fingers. Bend arm and gently pinch elbow.

Hands

Flatten hand and cut out a tiny triangle of paste on one side to form a mitten shape. Cut a small amount off the thumb and smooth to shape end. Indent a line half-way across the length of the hand, then in between each (three indents to form four fingers). When making tiny fingers, it is best not to cut right through, just indent. Curve fingers inwards.

Cut out and colour a rose calyx. Attach to the top of the arm to form a small cap-sleeve. Attach one arm under the body and one on top with the calyx brought over the top of the arm. Position the arms to look natural.

Wings

Tape together two quarter-length white wires (33g) leaving 3cm uncovered to form 'v' shape. Make two. Roll out flowerpaste very finely and leave to dry slightly. Place a small ball of flower paste at the base of each wire, squeeze firmly and roll back up to the tip of the wires. Place under plastic to keep soft. Flip over the rolled-out paste and cut out using Butterfly Wings. Cut out a small piece of paste where the butterfly body would be, to form two separate wings. Lay the paste-covered 'v' wires on the cut-out wing and press into position with the join of the 'v' where the body of the butterfly would be. Lay wing on face of Poppy Petal Veiner, cover with the back veiner and press very firmly. Cut off excess wire from tips of wings. Colour by brushing with powder colours. Tape together with wire-sides facing. Frill each wing with the JEM petal veiner. Dip into leaf glaze and while still wet, sprinkle a tiny amount of food-safe disco glitter.

Cut wires on stem of butterfly to 0.5cm. Make a hole with a cocktail stick between shoulders a short way down from neck. Insert wire from wings into the hole. Position wings to dry.

Make hair using royal icing and No.1 or No.1.5 piping tube. Pipe long curly hair flowing over the flower.

SweetPeaFairy

Use Mexican paste, or a mixture of Mexican and sugarpaste with a tiny amount of Paprika food colour paste for the head, arms and legs, Eucalyptus Green for the body.

Head

Make a smooth 1.5cm ball of Flesh-coloured Mexican paste.
Shape to form a short cone with a point.
Gently rub a small amount of cornflour onto the surface.
Put into the largest of the four Fairy Head moulds (Holly Products) with the point into the nose.
Lay a half-length of 18g wire on top the paste and push the paste and wire into the mould with the end of a small rolling pin.
Keeping the head in the mould, bring the spare paste together to form the back of the head and lift head out of mould.
Cut off excess paste with scissors.
Shape the neck by smoothing it down the wire.

Face

Paint facial features with very fine paintbrush, powder colours and alcohol;
• pearl white in the whole eye socket
• very thin dark brown curve for the top eyelid
• very thin brown curve for the eyebrow above the eye
• coloured iris - lavender. Paint a circle with the top slightly cut off by the eyelid
• pupil - a tiny circle of black in the centre of the iris
• dot of light - very tiny dot of white (best left out if you do not have a steady hand!)
• lips - soft dusky pink, paint a single line along between the lips - this looks much more delicate and is easier than painting separate lips.

Body

Form Mexican paste coloured with Eucalyptus Green into a smooth 2cm ball.
Use little finger to roll across the ball to form a waist.
Holding finger on top of the shoulder, push dogbone tool up to form arm socket. Push body up wire to head leaving a small amount of neck showing under head.
Pinch to form leg sockets.
Leave the wire long so that this fairy can sit on a mushroom.

Mushroom

Form a 3cm ball of Mexican paste.

Squash slightly and pinch out edge to form a 5cm circle fat in middle, thinner on edge.

On one face of circle mark lines radiating from the centre to appear like the gills of a mushroom.

Make an indentation in the centre of the circle on the same side with the large end of a dogbone tool or ball tool.

Dust that side with Nutkin Brown.

Dust the edge of the flat side with Autumn Leaf.

Make a sausage of Mexican paste 5cm long to form the mushroom stem.

Push the mushroom and stem up the wire under the body.

Legs

Make both legs at the same time to ensure they are the same size.
Make two smooth 1.5cm balls of Flesh-coloured Mexican paste and put one under plastic while working on the other.
Roll each ball to form long carrot-shape approximately the length of the head and body combined.

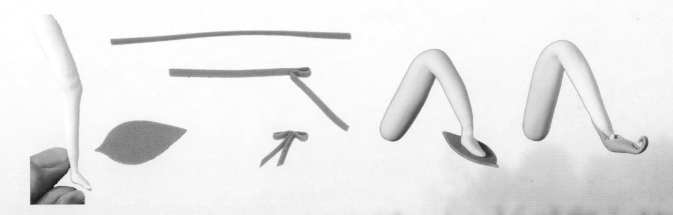

A short way from narrow end, roll between two fingers to form an indent for ankle. Half-way between ankle and top of thigh, roll between two fingers. Bend leg and pinch front of the knee. Bend the foot forward and pinch to form a heel.

Shoes

Make shoes by cutting out the small, or next size leaf cutter. Powder with chosen colour. Stick to feet with longest point longer than toes, short point coming up over heel and up leg. The long point can be rolled together gently to form a point and then curled up.

Stick legs into position with a dampened brush, knees bent and legs crossed.

Skirt

Cut out four sets of Sweet Pea petals from rolled-out flowerpaste to form the skirt. Powder colour each one. Frill each petal with a Jem petal veiner. Dampen around the waist. Stick Sweet Pea petals on to form a skirt, using largest petal for the first layer.

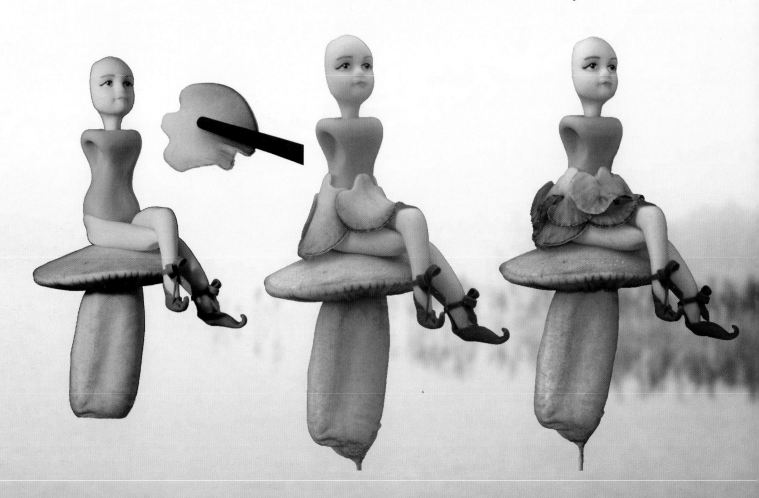

Waistcoat

Cut out at least five Periwinkle leaves (2.5cm) to form the waistcoat. Press into leaf veiner. Powder colour each one. I used Eucalyptus green.

Stick onto top of body, long point down over tops of petal skirt. Two on back, three on front. Make three tiny balls of paste and attach to the front of the waistcoat for buttons. Use a pin to mark the holes in the buttons.

Arms

Make both arms at the same time to ensure they are the same size. Make two smooth 1cm balls of Mexican paste coloured with Paprika food colour paste. Put one of them under plastic while working on the other. Roll each ball to form a long carrot-shape, slightly longer than the distance between the arm socket and the mushroom.

A short way from the narrow end, roll between two fingers to form an indent for the wrist. Half-way between the wrist and top of arm, roll between two fingers. Bend arm and gently pinch elbow.

Hands

Flatten hand and cut out a tiny triangle of paste on one side to form a mitten shape. Cut a small amount off the thumb and smooth to shape end. Indent a line half-way across the length of the hand, then in-between each (three indents to form four fingers). When shaping small fingers, it is best not to cut right through, just indent. Curve fingers inwards.

Cut out and colour a rose calyx to form a small cap-sleeve. Stick onto the arm socket ready for sticking to the top of the arm when it is attached. Stick arms into position, bringing petals of sleeve over top of arm.

Wings

Tape together two quarter-length white wires (33g) leaving 3cm uncovered to form 'v' shape. Make two. Roll out flowerpaste very finely and leave to dry slightly. Place a small ball of flowerpaste at the base of each wire, squeeze firmly and roll back up to the tip of the wires. Place under plastic to keep soft. Flip over the rolled-out paste and cut out using Butterfly Wings. Cut out a small piece of paste where the butterfly body would be, to form 2 separate wings. Lay the paste-covered 'v' wires on the cut-out wing and press into position with the join of the 'v' where the body of the butterfly would be. Lay wing on face of Poppy Petal Veiner, cover with the back veiner and press very firmly. Cut off excess wire from tips of wings. Colour by brushing with powder colours. Tape together with wire-sides facing. Frill each wing with the JEM Petal Veiner.
Dip into leaf glaze and while still wet dip edges of wings into food-safe glitter, or sprinkle with the glitter. Leave to dry for a few minutes.

When dry enough to handle, cut wires to 0.5cm. Make a small hole with a cocktail stick between shoulders a short way down from neck. Insert wire from wings into the hole. Position wings to dry.

Hair and Hat

Cut out the two different-shaped petals with a large Sweet Pea Cutter, colour as for the skirt and frill heavily with JEM Petal Veiner. Keep covered until ready to stick to hair.
Cut out tiny Calyx/Jasmine shape. Powder colour with Eucalyptus and keep covered.
Pipe hair with coloured royal icing using No.1 or No.1.5 piping tube, starting round the face and top of neck, then half-way up head, then top of head.

Stick Sweet Pea petals onto soft royal icing hair. The split petal closest to the hair, the wide petal on top of that, and finally the tiny calyx at the base of the petals at the back of her head.

Cut off excess wire allowing 3cm under mushroom stem.

Holly Elf

Snowball Base

Make a large 8cm snowball of sugarpaste (cake covering).
Surround it with some smaller balls of sugarpaste to look like snowballs. Stick them on with a small amount of water. For a frosty effect (not shown) either dust with edible pearl white powder, or sprinkle with edible white glitter. Put to one side to set.

Colour Mexican paste to a strong dark green for the body, arms and leaves. I used Spruce Green and small amount of Liquorice food colour paste(black).

Colour a small amount of Mexican paste with Christmas Red for the legs, hands and berries.

Head

Make a smooth 1.5cm ball of flesh-coloured Mexican paste.
Shape to form a short cone with a point.
Gently rub a small amount of cornflour on the surface.
Put into the Fairy/Elf head mould (Holly Products) with the point into the nose.
Lay a 10cm length of 18g wire on top the paste and push the paste and wire into the mould with the end of a small rolling pin.
Keeping the head in the mould bring the spare paste together to form the back of the head and lift head out of mould and press together.
Cut off excess paste with scissors.
Cut off the neck, leaving just the head on the wire.

Face

Paint facial features with very fine paintbrush, powder colours and alcohol:

      pearl white in the whole eye socket
      very thin dark brown curve for the top eyelid
      very thin brown curve for the eyebrow above the eye
      coloured iris - foliage green. Paint a circle with the top slightly cut off by the eyelid
      pupil - a tiny circle of black in the centre of the iris
      dot of light - Very tiny dot of white (best left out if you do not have a steady hand!)
      lips - very pale dusky pink, paint a single line along between the lips (remember that this is a little boy elf, so keep the lips pale)

Hair

Paint a wispy fringe with brown powder mixed with alcohol.

Hat

Form a ball of dark green Mexican Paste approximately the same size as the head.
Roll it to form a pointed cone.
At the wide end make a hollow by pressing in fingers. It will look a little bit like a golf tee.
Gently press round edge of hollow, big enough to fit over back of his head.
Pinch edge towards one side of the hollow to form a flattened point.
Try the size of the hat, pinching out more if necessary before dampening to stick the hat onto back of head with the longer flat piece sticking round the neck under the chin.
Curl the pointed tip, and put a small dip in the end of the point with a ball tool to help the berry to stick on later.
With a Dresden Tool, tuck the paste back slightly where the ears will be going.

Ears

Two tiny balls of flesh-coloured Mexican paste, each formed to a sharp point. Stick to side of head and press in firmly with Dresden tool. This will form the hollow for the ear at the same time as sticking it firmly to the head.

Body

Form Mexican paste coloured dark green into a smooth 2cm ball.

Use little finger to roll across the ball to form a waist.

Holding finger on top of the shoulder, push Dogbone Tool in and up to form arm socket.

Pinch to form leg sockets. Push body up wire to head leaving a small amount of neck showing under head.

Cut wire to the depth of sugarpaste "snowball".

Push wire into the "snowball", making sure that the elf is sitting straight up.

(The wire will stay in position better if bent, but 18g wire is not very easy to bend when it is short).

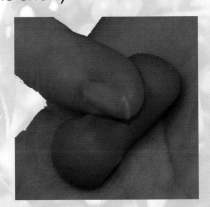

Legs

Make both legs at the same time to ensure they are the same size. Make two smooth 1.5cm balls of Mexican paste coloured with red paste colour and put one under plastic sheet while working on the other. Roll each to form long carrot-shape approximately length of the head and body combined. A short way from narrow end, roll between two fingers to form an indent for ankle. Half-way between ankle and top of thigh, roll between two fingers. Bend leg and pinch front of knee. Bend the foot forward and pinch to form a heel. Foot must be much smaller than cutter used for shoe. Bend tightly at knees.

Shoes

Roll out dark green Mexican paste very thinly and leave for a few minutes to dry. Turn over and cut out at least two small/medium Holly Leaves.

Stick onto the sole of the foot with the stem part coming up the back of the heels and leg to look like ankle boots. Gently roll tip of the leaf at toe-end to form a point.

Attach legs to base of body and position legs angled out to look crossed-legged.

Finish shoes by adding a small red berry on the toe-end of the shoe.

Clothes

Roll out dark green Mexican paste very thinly and leave for a few minutes to dry.

Turn over and cut out at least nine small/medium holly leaves.

Press in Holly Leaf Veiner (or Hydrangea Leaf Veiner).

Stick stem-ends of each leaf round waist to form a 'skirt'.

Make enough small 0.25cm red berries to stick around waist forming a belt. Stick on by dampening around the waist, pick up each berry by stabbing it with a cocktail stick, press the stick up against the waist, and help the berry gently off the stick.

Hands

Using red Mexican paste make two small 0.5cm balls for the hands. Roll each ball to form a cone. The round end will form the fingers, the pointed end will stick in the sleeve. Flatten hand and cut out a tiny triangle of paste on one side to form a mitten shape. Indent a line half-way across the length of the hand, then in between each (three indents form four fingers). When shaping small fingers, it is best not to cut right through, just indent. Curve fingers inwards. Make a left and right hand. Keep the hands covered while you make the arms.

Arms

Start the same way as for making the legs, but with a 1cm ball of dark green Mexican paste. Make both arms at the same time to ensure they are the same size. Put one of them under a plastic sheet while working on the other. Roll each to form long carrot-shape, slightly longer than the shoulder to the snowball base. At the narrow end, make small hollow for his hand with small Dogbone tool. Half-way between the wrist and top of arm roll between two fingers to form the elbow. Bend arm and gently pinch elbow. Cut out two small Holly Leaves from rolled-out dark green Mexican paste. Stick each Holly Leaf into the dampened, hollow end of sleeve with the Dogbone Tool. Stick the hand into the hollow, making sure it is the right way round. Stick arms in position by dampening the arm-socket with water.

Collar

Cut out three small Holly Leaves from rolled-out dark green Mexican Paste. Stick into position. Make two or three tiny red balls to stick down in a row under the neck for buttons.

Wings

Tape together two quarter-length white wires (33g) leaving 3cm uncovered to form 'v' shape. Make two. Roll out flowerpaste very finely and leave to dry slightly. Place a small ball of flowerpaste at the base of each wire, squeeze firmly and roll back up to the tip of the wires. Place under plastic to keep soft.

Flip over the rolled-out paste and cut out Butterfly wings. Lay the paste-covered 'v' wires on the cut-out wing and press into position with the join of the 'v' where the body of the butterfly would be. Lay wing on face of Poppy Petal Veiner, cover with the back veiner and press very firmly. Cut off excess wire from tips of wings. Colour by brushing with powder colours. Tape together with wire-sides facing. Frill each wing with the JEM Petal Veiner.

Dip into leaf glaze and, while still wet, dip edges of wings into food-safe glitter, or sprinkle with the glitter. Leave to dry for a few minutes.
When dry enough to handle, cut wires to 0.5cm. Make a small hole with a cocktail stick between shoulders a short way down from neck. Insert wire from wings into the hole. Position wings to dry.

Attach berry to point of hat.
Finish by painting the leaves and berries with full-strength Confectioners Varnish, using cotton bud or old thin paintbrush, carefully avoiding his face and ears.

NarcissusFairy

Use Mexican paste, or a mixture of Mexican and sugarpaste with a tiny amount of Paprika food colour paste for the head arms and legs, White for the body.

Head

Make a smooth 1.5cm ball of Flesh-coloured Mexican paste.
Shape to form a short cone with a point. Gently rub a small amount of cornflour over the surface. Put into the Small Child Head mould (Holly Products) with the point into the nose.
Lay a half length 18g wire on top the paste and push the paste and wire into the mould with the end of a small rolling pin. Keeping the head in the mould bring the spare paste together to form the back of the head and lift head out of mould.

Cut off excess paste with scissors.
Shape the neck by smoothing it down the wire.

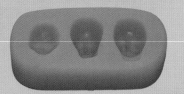

Face

Paint facial features with very fine paintbrush, powder colours and alcohol.

• pearl white in the whole eye socket
• very thin dark brown curve for the top eyelid
• very thin brown curve for the eyebrow above the eye
• coloured iris - brown. Paint a circle with the top slightly cut off by the eyelid
• pupil - a tiny circle of black in the centre of the iris
• dot of light - Very tiny dot of white (best left out if you do not have a steady hand!)
• lips - soft dusky pink, paint a single line along between the lips - this looks much more delicate, and is easier than painting separate lips.

Body

Form White Mexican paste into a smooth 2cm ball.
Use little finger to roll across the ball to form a waist.
Holding finger on top of the shoulder, push Dogbone Tool in and up to form arm socket.
Pinch to form leg sockets. Push body up wire to head leaving a small amount of neck showing under head.

Cut wire to required length - either

• fill a posy-pick with sugarpaste, push into cake, then push the base wire of the fairy into the posy-pick

• or push shortened straight wire into large ball of sugarpaste or oasis, making sure that fairy is sitting.

Legs

Make both legs at the same time to ensure they are the same size. Make two smooth 1.5cm balls with Flesh-coloured Mexican paste and put one under plastic while working on the other. Roll each ball to form long carrot-shape approximately the length of the head and body combined. A short way from narrow end, roll between two fingers to form an indent for ankle. Half-way between ankle and top of thigh, roll between two fingers. Bend leg and pinch front of the knee. Bend the foot forward and pinch to form a heel. Stick legs into position with a dampened paintbrush, knees bent and legs to one side.

Skirt

Cut out six petals (3cm Periwinkle leaf) from rolled-out flowerpaste to form the skirt.
Press each petal in an Alstromeria Veiner.
Thin the edges of each petal with a Jem Petal Veiner.
Dampen round the waist.
Stick petals on to form a skirt, narrow end to the body.

Arms

Make both arms at the same time to ensure they are the same size. Make two smooth 1cm balls of Flesh-coloured Mexican paste. Put one of them under plastic while working on the other. Roll each ball to form long carrot-shape, slightly longer than the distance between the arm socket and the surface the fairy is sitting on. A short way from the narrow end, roll between two fingers to form an indent for the wrist. Half-way between the wrist and top of arm roll between two fingers. Bend arm and gently pinch elbow.

Hands

Flatten hand and cut out a tiny triangle of paste on one side to form a mitten shape. Cut a small amount off the thumb and smooth to shape the end. Indent a line half-way across the length of the hand, then in between each (three indents to form four fingers). When shaping small fingers it is best not to cut right through- just indent. Curve fingers inwards. Make sure that you make a left and right hand. Attach arms to the arm sockets, and position them while still soft.

Collar

Cut out two Medium Carnations from rolled-out flowerpaste..
Colour by brushing with Tangerine Powder.
Frill firmly over edge with JEM Petal Veiner.
Paint the edges with Burgundy powder mixed with alcohol.
Cut out centre with 1cm Circle Cutter.
Cut a single line in the frill, and attach around neck with the join at the back of her neck.

Wings

Tape together two quarter-length white wires (33g) leaving 3cm uncovered to form 'v' shape. Make two.
Roll out flowerpaste very finely and leave to dry slightly. Place a small ball of flowerpaste at the base of each wire, squeeze firmly and roll back up to the tip of the wires.
Place under plastic to keep soft.

Flip over the rolled-out paste and cut out using Butterfly Wings. Lay the paste-covered 'v' wires on the cut-out wing and press into position with the join of the 'v' where the body of the butterfly would be.
Lay wing on face of Poppy Petal Veiner, cover with the back veiner and press very firmly.
Cut off excess wire from tips of wings.

Colour by brushing with Tangerine powder.
Tape wings together with wire-sides facing.
Frill each wing with the JEM Petal Veiner. Dip into leaf glaze and while still wet, dip edges of wings into Food-safe glitter, or sprinkle with the glitter. Leave to dry for a few minutes.

Cut wires to 0.5cm.
Make a hole with a cocktail stick between shoulders a short way down from neck.
Insert wire from wings into the hole.
Position wings to dry.

Cut out tiny Plunger Blossoms from rolled-out flowerpaste, two for each foot.
Colour by brushing with Tangerine powder.
Frill edges.
Stick two on top of each foot to form a pom-pom.
Paint edges with Burgundy powder mixed with alcohol.

Mini Narcissus

Cut out tiny Six-petal Flower cutter and a tiny Plunger Blossom from rolled-out flowerpaste. Powder colour the Blossom with Tangerine and frill it. Paint the edges of the frilled centre with burgundy powder mixed with alcohol. Attach to the centre of the Six-petal flower. Leave to one side until the hair has been piped.

Hair

Pipe hair with coloured royal icing using No.1 or No.1.5 piping tube, starting round the face and top of neck, then half-way up head, then top of head.
Stick the mini narcissus onto soft royal icing hair.

Primrose Fairy

Primrose Leaf Base

Roll fine flowerpaste - allow surface to dry.
Take a small ball of flowerpaste and insert a dry white 33g wire a distance equal to the length of the Primrose Leaf cutter. Squeeze firmly and roll back up to the tip of the wire. Place under a plastic sheet while preparing the rest of the wires, making one for each leaf. Flip rolled-out paste over, cut out at least seven leaves.

Press a paste-covered wire on each leaf, right to the tip of the leaf.
Lay each leaf on a Primrose Leaf veiner, wire side onto the back face of the veiner, helping to form the vein on the back. Press very firmly with the other half of the veiner. This will fix the wire to the leaf. Repeat with the remaining leaves. Colour each leaf by brushing with Foliage Green powder. Thin the lobed edges of each leaf with a Jem petal veiner. Dip the leaves into Leaf Glaze and blot straight-away on tissue. Shape each leaf by pinching the back vein for the length of the leaf, then curling the lobed edges over.
Tape together with quarter-width florist tape as soon as the glaze has evaporated to form a bunch which can be opened to form a flat circle. Put to one side until the fairy head and body have been made.

Use Mexican paste, or a mixture of Mexican and sugarpaste with a tiny amount of Paprika food colour paste for the head and arms, Christmas Green for the body and legs.

Head

Make a smooth 1.5cm ball of Flesh-coloured Mexican paste.
Shape to form a short cone with a point.
Gently rub a small amount of cornflour over the surface.
Put into the Fairy/Elf head mould (Holly Products) with the point into the nose.
Lay a half-length 18g wire on top the paste and push the paste and wire into the mould with the end of a small rolling pin.
Keeping the head in the mould, bring the spare paste together to form the back of the head and lift head out of mould.
Cut off excess paste with scissors.
Shape the neck by smoothing it down the wire.

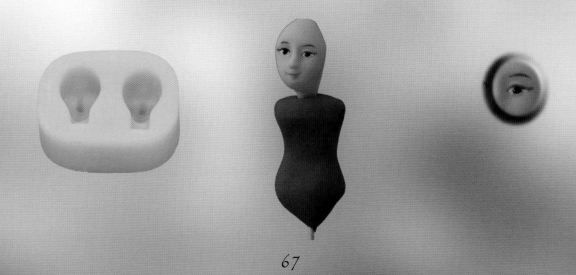

Face

Paint facial features with very fine paintbrush, powder colours and alcohol.

- pearl white in the whole eye socket
- very thin dark brown curve for the top eyelid
- very thin brown curve for the eyebrow above the eye
- coloured iris - blue. Paint a circle with the top slightly cut off at the top by the eyelid
- pupil - a tiny circle of black in the centre of the iris
- dot of light - Very tiny dot of white (best left out if you do not have a steady hand!)
- lips - soft dusky pink, paint a single line along between the lips - this looks much more delicate and is easier than painting separate lips.

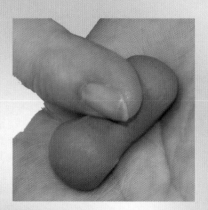  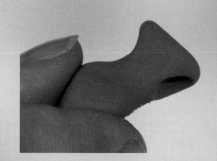

Body

Form Green Mexican paste into a smooth 2cm ball.
Use little finger to roll across the ball to form a waist.
Holding finger on top of the shoulder, push Dogbone tool in and up to form arm socket.
Pinch to form leg sockets. Push body up wire to head leaving a small amount of neck showing under head.

Tape the wire from the body to the stem of the Primrose Leaves, so that the fairy is sitting in the middle of them.

Cut wire to required length - either
• fill a posy-pick with sugarpaste, push into cake, then push the base wire of the fairy into the posy pick
• or push shortened straight wire into large ball of sugarpaste or oasis, making sure that fairy is sitting.

Legs

Make both legs at the same time to ensure they are the same size.
Make two smooth 1.5cm balls with Green Mexican paste and put one under plastic while working on the other.
Roll each ball to form long carrot-shape approximately the combined length of the head and body.
A short way from narrow end, roll between two fingers to form an indent for ankle.
Half-way between ankle and top of thigh, roll between two fingers.
Bend leg and pinch front of heel.
Bend foot forward and pinch to form heel.
Foot must be much smaller than cutter used for shoe.

Shoes

Cut out two small Periwinkle Leaves and two tiny hearts from rolled-out flowerpaste. Colour by brushing with Primrose Powder. Dampen, stick to base of foot, stick pointed end up over heel. Bring sides together. It can also be cut if too long. Stick tiny Heart on top of foot to form front of shoe.

Stick legs to soft body dampened with water, positioning them with knees bent. Dampen between the legs with a little water to stick them together.

Skirt

Cut out five heart-shape petals (2cm) from rolled-out flowerpaste to form the skirt. Colour by brushing with Primrose Powder. Thin each petal with a Jem petal veiner. Dampen round the waist. Stick petals on to form a skirt, narrow end to the body.

Waistcoat

Cut out at least five Periwinkle leaves to form the waistcoat. Press into Poppy Petal veiner. Colour each one by brushing with Foliage Green.
Stick on to the body with the points coming down over the top of the petal skirt, long point down.

Sleeve

Cut out a Primrose Flower from rolled-out flowerpaste to form a small sleeve. Stick it onto the arm socket ready for sticking to the top of the arm when it is attached.

Arms

Make both arms at the same time to ensure they are the same size.

Make two smooth 1cm balls of Flesh-coloured Mexican paste. Put one of them under plastic while working on the other.

Roll each ball to form long carrot-shape, slightly longer than the distance between the arm socket and the leaves the fairy is sitting on.

A short way from the narrow end, roll between two fingers to form an indent for the wrist.

Half-way between the wrist and top of arm, roll between two fingers. Bend arm and gently pinch elbow.

Hands

Flatten hand and cut out a tiny triangle of paste on one side to form a mitten shape. Cut a small amount off the thumb and smooth to shape end. Indent a line half-way across the length of the hand, then in between each (three indents to form four fingers). When shaping small fingers, it is best not to cut right through, just indent. Curve fingers inwards. Make sure that you make a left and right hand. Attach arms to the arm sockets, and position them while still soft.

Wings

Tape together two quarter-length white wires (33g) leaving 3cm uncovered to form 'v' shape. Make two.
Roll out flowerpaste very finely and leave to dry slightly. Place a small ball of flowerpaste at the base of each wire, squeeze firmly and roll back up to the tip of the wires.
Place under plastic to keep soft.

Flip over the rolled-out paste and cut out using Butterfly Wings. Lay the paste-covered 'v' wires on the cut-out wing and press into position with the join of the 'v' where the body of the butterfly would be.
Lay wing on face of Poppy Petal Veiner, cover with the back veiner and press very firmly.
Cut off excess wire from tips of wings.

Colour by brushing the wings with powder colour.
Tape together with wire-sides facing.
Frill each wing with the JEM petal veiner. Dip into leaf glaze. Leave to dry for a few minutes.

Cut wires to 0.5cm.
Make a small hole with a cocktail stick between shoulders a short way down from neck.
Insert wire from wings into the hole.
Position wings to dry.

Hat

Roll out flowerpaste to form a 'Mexican Hat', cut out a primrose. Powder with Primrose. Thin each petal of the flower with the Jem petal veiner. Form a nice curved point on the tail.

Hair

Pipe hair with coloured royal icing using No.1, or No.1.5 tube, starting round the face and top of neck, then half-way up head, then top of head.
Stick the primrose flower onto soft royal icing hair.

Daffodil Fairy

Use Mexican paste, or a mixture of Mexican and Sugarpaste with a tiny amount of Paprika food colour paste for the head and arms, Melon yellow for the body and legs.

Head

Make a smooth 1.5cm ball of Flesh-coloured Mexican paste.
Shape to form a short cone with a point.
Gently rub a small amount of cornflour over the surface.
Put into the largest of the four Fairy Head moulds (Holly Products) with the point into the nose.
Lay a half-length 18g wire on top the paste and push the paste and wire into the mould with the end of a small rolling pin.
Keeping the head in the mould, bring the spare paste together to form the back of the head and lift head out of mould.
Cut off excess paste with scissors.
Shape the neck by smoothing it down the wire.

Paint facial features with very fine paintbrush, powder colours and alcohol:
• pearl white in the whole eye socket
• very thin dark brown curve for the top eyelid
• very thin brown curve for the eyebrow above the eye
• coloured iris - blue. Paint a circle with the top slightly cut off by the eyelid
• pupil - a tiny circle of black in the centre of the iris
• dot of light - very tiny dot of white (best left out if you do not have a steady hand!)
• lips - soft dusky pink, paint a single line along between the lips - this looks much more delicate, and is easier than painting separate lips.

Body

Form Mexican paste coloured with Melon yellow into a smooth ball approximately 2cm.
Use little finger to roll across the ball to form a waist.
Holding finger on top of the shoulder, push Dogbone tool up to form arm socket.
Pinch to form leg sockets.
Push body up wire to head leaving a small amount of neck showing under head, making sure that the wire comes out through one of the leg sockets.

Leave the wire long so that this fairy can stand.

Legs

Make both legs at the same time to ensure they are the same size.
Make two smooth, 1.5cm pieces of Mexican paste coloured with Melon yellow and put one under plastic while working on the other.

1) Push the ball for the first leg up the main wire to about 2cm from leg socket.
2) Roll ball to form long carrot-shape 7cm. As you roll the leg, it pushes up the wire to join the body.
3) A short way from narrow end, roll between two fingers to form an indent for ankle.
4) Half-way between ankle and top of thigh roll between two fingers to form knee. This leg stays straight because of the strong wire.

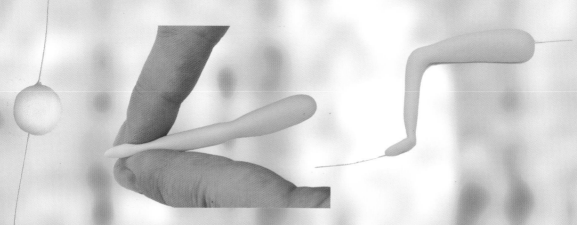

5) Pinch the paste away from the wire to form a foot and pinch to form a heel.
6) Repeat steps 1-5 but using a separate 33g wire to form the second leg.
7) Bend the knee.
8) At the thigh-end bend the wire to form a hook. Push into the leg socket and stick in position with water.
9) Attach the 33g wire, which sticks out from under the foot to the main stem with half-width florist tape, making sure that the second foot is pointing down close to the first or slightly behind, and the knee is bent.

Shoes

Paint ballet shoes with pearlised powder colour mixed with alcohol.

Underskirt

Roll out paste very thinly and leave for a few minutes to dry.
Turn over and cut out using Garrett frill with medium middle cutter.
Powder colour with Lemon yellow.
Frill whole depth of skirt with Jem veiner tool, not just the edge.

Cut frill in half, it makes it easier to attach.
Gather along non-frilled edge, to fit half way round waist from side to side. Stick the back of skirt first.
Gather second piece and form front of skirt (cut edge should not be shown).

Roll out flowerpaste very thinly and leave for a few minutes to dry.
Turn over, cut out six large Periwinkle Leaves.
Press into Alstromeria or Poppy veiner.

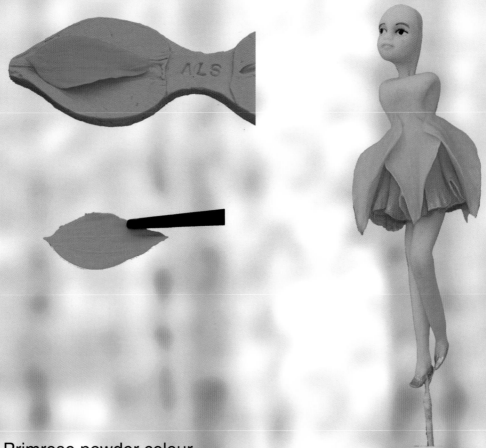

Colour with Primrose powder colour.
Dampen round the waist to stick on petals, evenly spaced to form over-skirt.
Prop up petals away from under-skirt with small pieces of cotton wool (remove later when petals are set).
Cut out two flowers using a small 3cm six-petal cutter.
Colour by brushing with Primrose powder. Soften shape of petals with Jem petal veiner.
Moisten arm sockets and attach flower, leaving flat and open for arm to be attached.

Arms

Make both arms at the same time to ensure they are the same size.

Make two smooth 1cm balls of flesh coloured Mexican paste and put one of them under plastic while working on the other.

Roll each ball to form a 5.5cm long carrot-shape.

A short way from the narrow end, roll between two fingers to form an indent for the wrist.

Half-way between the wrist and top of arm roll between two fingers to form the elbow.

Bend arm and gently pinch elbow.

Hands

Flatten hand and cut out a tiny triangle of paste on one side to form a mitten shape.

Cut a small amount off the thumb and smooth to shape end.

Fingers

Indent a line half-way across the length of the hand, then in between each (three indents form four fingers). When shaping small fingers, it is best not to cut right through, just indent. Curve fingers inwards.

Attach arms to dampened arm sockets bringing petals around top of arm. Position arms, sticking where necessary.

Cut out four or five tiny six-petal flowers from rolled-out sugarpaste. Colour by brushing with Primrose Powder.

Place each flower over top of Jem petal veiner and press petals to form closed flower.

Dampen round neck and attach each flower by pushing in with the veiner tool, to form a ruffled collar.

Wings

Tape together two quarter-length white wires (33g) leaving 3cm uncovered to form 'v' shape. Make two.

Roll out flowerpaste very finely and leave to dry slightly.

Place a small ball of flowerpaste at the base of each wire, squeeze firmly and roll back up to the tip of the wires. Place under plastic sheet to keep soft.

Flip over the rolled-out paste and cut out Butterfly wings. Lay the paste-covered 'v' wires on the cut-out wing and press into position with the join of the 'v' where the body of the butterfly would be. Lay wings on face of Poppy Petal Veiner, cover with the back veiner and press very firmly. Cut off excess wire from tips of wings.

Powder with Primrose colour at body end. Tape together with wire-sides facing.

Frill each wing with the JEM petal veiner.

Dip in leaf glaze, lightly sprinkle wings with food-safe glitter while glaze is still wet, and leave to dry. Cut wires to 0.5cm.

Make a hole between shoulders a short way down from neck with cocktail stick.

Insert wire from wings into the hole.

Position wings to dry.

Hair

Pipe hair with royal icing coloured with a tiny amount of Melon yellow. Pipe with No.1 or No.1.5 piping tube from hair line around the face first.
Attach two or three tiny six-petal flowers to the damp hair.

Base- To Display Finished Fairy

• fill a posy-pick with sugarpaste, push into cake, then push the base wire of the fairy into the posy pick
• or push shortened straight wire into large ball of sugarpaste or oasis, making sure that fairy is standing straight up, then decorate with flowers and leaves
• or bend wire under foot to form a stand and cover with sugarpaste.

Autumn Fairy

Start by making a branch with autumn leaves of your choice - I made hazel using a nut mould, calyx, large rose leaf cutter and hazel leaf veiner.

Use Mexican paste, or a mixture of Mexican and sugarpaste with a tiny amount of Paprika food colour paste for the head and arms, stronger Paprika for the body and legs.

Head

Make a smooth 1.5cm ball of paste.
Shape to form a short cone with a point.
Gently rub a small amount of cornflour over the surface.
Put into the Fairy/Elf head mould (Holly Products) with the point into the nose.

Lay a half length 18g wire on top the paste and push the paste and wire into the mould with the end of a small rolling pin.
Keeping the head in the mould bring the spare paste together to form the back of the head and lift head out of mould.
Cut off excess paste with scissors.
Shape the neck by smoothing it down the wire.

Paint facial features with very fine paintbrush, powder colours and alcohol
• pearl white in the whole eye socket
• very thin dark brown curve for the top eyelid
• very thin brown curve for the eyebrow above the eye
• coloured iris - brown. Paint a circle with the top slightly cut off at the top by the eyelid.
• pupil - a tiny circle of black in the centre of the iris
• dot of light - a <u>very tiny </u>dot of white (best left out if you do not have a steady hand!)
• lips - soft dusky pink, paint a single line along between the lips - this looks much more delicate, and is easier than painting separate lips.

Body

Form Mexican paste coloured strongly with Paprika into a smooth 2cm ball.
Use little finger to roll across the ball to form a waist.
Holding finger on top of the shoulder, push dogbone tool up to form arm socket. Pinch to form leg sockets.
Push body up wire to head leaving a small amount of neck showing under head, making sure that the wire comes out through one of the leg sockets.
Leave the wire long so that this fairy can stand.

 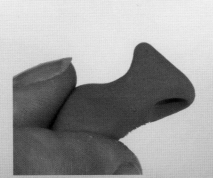 

Legs

Make both legs at the same time to ensure they are the same size.
Make two smooth 1.5cm pieces of Flesh-coloured Mexican paste.
Put one under plastic while working on the other.

1) Push the ball for the first leg up the main wire to about 2cm from leg socket.
2) Roll to form a 7cm long carrot-shape. As you roll the leg, it pushes up the wire to join the body.
3) A short way from narrow end, roll between two fingers to form an indent for ankle.
4) Half way between ankle and top of thigh, roll between two fingers to form knee. This leg stays straight because of the strong wire.
5) Pinch the paste away from the wire to form a foot and pinch to form a heel.
6) Repeat steps 1-5 but using a separate 33g wire to form the second leg.
7) Bend the knee.

At the thigh end bend the wire to form a hook. Push into the leg socket and stick in position with water.
Attach the 33g wire, which sticks out from under the foot, to the main stem with quarter-width florist tape, making sure that the second foot is pointing down close to the first or slightly behind, and the knee is bent.

Ankle boots

Cut out four small rose leaves. Press in Garden Rose Leaf veiner. Colour with Autumn Gold Powder. Stick the leaves under the feet, the point up the back of the leg. Then stick the second leaves on top of the feet. Cut off spare paste with small sharp scissors.

Tape the wire under the fairy's feet to either the branch made earlier with wires and Twig coloured florist tape, leaves and nuts. Alternatively you could attach her to a real, dried branch.

Skirt

Roll out paste very thinly and leave for a few minutes to dry. Turn over, cut out at least six medium Oak Leaves. Press into Oak or Hydrangea veiner. Colour with Autumn Gold powder colour. Dampen round the waist to stick on leaves.

Waistcoat

Cut out two medium Maple Leaves.
Colour with Burgundy powder. Attach to the body, the stem end at the neck, and the points of the leaf down over the top of the skirt. Leave the points of the leaf clear of the arm sockets, so that they can be stuck to the arms when they are attached.

Arms

If you would like your fairy to be holding the branch, a 33g wire inside the arm will help support it and make it stronger. If you want to make fingers, leave it until the hand is attached to the branch, then mark out the fingers with a sharp pointed knife.

Make both arms at the same time to ensure they are the same size.
Make two smooth 1cm balls of Flesh-coloured Mexican paste and put one of them under plastic while working on the other.
Insert a half-length 33g wire into each ball of paste, equal length of wire on either side of the ball.
Roll each ball to form a 5.5cm long carrot-shape.
A short way from the narrow end, roll between two fingers to form an indent for the wrist.
Half-way between the wrist and top of arm, roll between two fingers. Bend arm and gently pinch elbow.

Cut the wire at the shoulder-end to 1cm, bend to form a short hook and stick the arm to the arm socket, dampened with a little water. Position arms, winding the wire at the hand-end round the branch a couple of times. Cut off excess wire. Position the points of the Maple Leaf at the top of the arms.

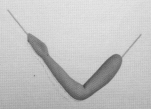

Wings

Tape together two quarter-length white wires (33g) leaving 3cm uncovered to form 'v' shape. Make two.

Roll out flowerpaste very finely and leave to dry slightly.

Place a small ball of flowerpaste at the base of each wire, squeeze firmly and roll back up to the tip of the wires. Place under plastic to keep soft.

Flip over the rolled-out paste and cut out butterfly wings.

Lay the paste-covered 'v' wires on the cut-out wing and press into position with the join of the 'v' where the body of the butterfly would be.

Lay on face of Poppy Petal Veiner, cover with the back veiner and press very firmly.

Cut off excess wire from tips of wings.

Powder colour with Burgundy at body end.

Tape together with wire-sides facing.

Frill each wing with the JEM petal veiner.

Dip in leaf glaze, dip edges of wings with food-safe glitter while glaze is still wet, and leave to dry. Cut wires to 0.5cm.

Make a small hole between shoulders a short way down from neck with cocktail stick.

Insert wire from wings into the hole.

Position wings to dry.

Hair

Pipe hair with royal icing coloured with Dark brown.
Pipe with No.1 or No.1.5 tube from hair line around the face first.

Base- To Display Finished Fairy

• fill a posy-pick with sugarpaste, push into cake, then push the base wire of the fairy into the posy-pick
• or push shortened straight wire into large ball of sugarpaste or oasis, making sure that fairy is standing straight up, then decorate with autumn leaves
• or bend wire under foot to form a stand and cover with sugarpaste.

Mexican Paste Recipe

227g/8oz icing sugar
3x 5ml teaspoons gum tragacanth
6x 5ml teaspoons water
Stir icing sugar and gum tragacanth together. Mix water in with fingers. Turn mixture out onto worktop and knead until pliable- if too sticky add more icing sugar, if too crumbly add a few drops of water. Store in a plastic bag overnight (not in a fridge). It can be coloured with paste food colours. Mexican paste can be frozen. Sugarpaste can be added 50:50 to the Mexican paste to use for moulds and flowers. Use small amount of vegetable oil/fat on workboard for rolling out finely for petals and leaves.

Visit www.patchworkcutters.co.uk for step-bystep pictures.

Classes, Demonstrations and Workshops

I regularly hold small, one-day classes for many different aspects of Sugarcraft. I provide you with all the equipment and materials you need to complete each project in one day.
My Website www.franklysweet.co.uk has listings of current classes, or you could choose to be updated regularly by email.

I also demonstrate and teach at workshops to branches of the British Sugarcraft Guild, National Sugarart Association and other sugarcraft clubs and businesses. Please contact me for details.

Other book titles by Frances McNaughton

Modelling Fancy Dress Babies, published 2009 by Frankly Sweet Publications

Sugar Animals - Twenty to Make, published 2009 by Search Press

Cup Cakes - Twenty to Make, published 2009 by Search Press

Sugar Fairies - Twenty to Make, published 2010 by Search Press

Useful Addresses

ALL PRODUCTS USED IN THIS BOOK ARE AVAILABLE BY
ORDERING DIRECT FROM ME THROUGH MY WEBSHOP
www.franklysweet.co.uk

EMAIL; fran.mac@btinternet.com OR frances.mcnaughton@gmail.com

FAIRY HEAD MOULDS;
HOLLY PRODUCTS, PRIMROSE COTTAGE, CHURCH WALK,
NORTON-IN-HALES,SHROPSHIRE,TF9 4QT

WHOLESALE SUGARCRAFT SUPPLIER TO RETAIL OUTLETS
GUY PAUL & CO LTD, PO BOX 522, AMERSHAM, HP6 6ZN

FLORIST WIRES AND TAPES
HAMILWORTH, CAMPBELLS MILL, ST GEORGES ROAD, NEW MILLS, HIGH PEAK SK22 4JZ

BRITISH SUGARCRAFT GUILD, WELLINGTON HOUSE, MESSETER PLACE,
ELTHAM, LONDON,SE9 5DP

NATIONAL SUGARART ASSOCIATION 0208 777 4445